The Darkness Above

Selected Poems
1968 – 2002

by Donald Lev

CRS Red Hill OUTLOUDBOOKS

PO Box 86 Claryville, New York 12725

Dedicated to Bob Richards, and in loving memory
of Enid Dame (1943-2003)

Special thanks to Michal Heron for her patient and tireless
efforts to bring this volume to fruition, and also to Theo
Chewiwi and Reyna Chewiwi for their efforts. Thanks to
Robert and Ursula Garrett for their work on the design
and production of a handsome book.

CRS OUTLOUDBOOKS/RED HILL BOOKS
Managing Editor: Reyna Chewiwi

Book design, cover photo and typography
by Garrett-Waldmeyer Int'l. Inc.

Previously published book cover designs:
Part 3, Ron Arico; Part 4, Chris Pelletiere;
Part 5, Brett Rutherford; Parts 6 & 8, Dan Smythe;
Part 7, Jenny Tango; Part 9, Patricia Fillingham;
Part 10, Garrett-Waldmeyer.

The Darkness Above

Selected Poems
1968 – 2002

by Donald Lev

Preface

Donald Lev's poetry is sublime. It catches you off guard. Though seemingly so simple and direct — it goes on to awaken depths in us all. Donald is an original voice among the many who, though heralded, are merely standard. His message is clear, poignant, often deeply comedic, yet inspiring in a time when slickness has become the norm.

Poetry still flourishes because it helps keep some sort of sensibility and offers peace of mind in a time of distress and foolishness. To endure, we need the power of original voices of poetry, music, art and good sense — commodities always short in supply and all but hidden unless the voices in Donald's poems are raised and made available to everyone.

However times are, Donald Lev's poetry will bring joy, laughter and understanding to those wily folk who pick up a book of his poems for the sheer pleasure of searching for good. Save yourself and send others to Donald's poetry, read it all...but not all at once. Take your time with these rich, splendid poems.

The purpose of this book is to celebrate Donald Lev for his observation and insight into being alive. Here, in this volume of selected poems, is the essence of a life lived fully and forever ours to behold.

Bob Richards

Table of Contents

Prologue

Part One
HYN 4
From HYN (1968)

Part Two
A String of Beads For Maxine 10
From A STRING OF BEADS FOR MAXINE (1971)

Part Three
Peculiar Merriment 18
From PECULIAR MERRIMENT (1973)

Part Ten
Yesterday's News

From YESTERDAY'S NEWS (2002)

Prologue

AUTOBIOGRAPHY

years went by, nothing
seemed to improve
expectation after
expectation
dropped from the psyche like
snakeskins
what was left in this
pause in time
a rime of
serpents and
grasses
calms, storms, rains, sunshine
heat cold
love, and the funnels between loves
I heard a whisper somewhere next to me
it was the holy gold robed being that only I can see
with the eyes of typewriter keys
it whispered of a finer reality

From *Peculiar Merriment*

PERPLEXITY

occasionally
a black
numeral denoting
half-infinity
makes its appearance on
this threadbare white cloth i
use to cover
the cage of my crazy
pet archangel
otherwise she's no trouble...

From *Peculiar Merriment*

1

THE MESSENGER

I returned to myself just in time to turn off the alarm. My astral feet were as sore from walking the streets all night as my natural ones were from walking the same streets the day before, so I had trouble pulling my boots over my swollen ankles. But I got them on anyway and got to work almost on time.

I'm a messenger. On both this and the astral plane. And holding two jobs isn't easy. I'd leave this one, but unfortunately for the astral work you must have a body to leave, otherwise it's no go.

So next time you see a messenger talking to himself (it may or may not be me), remember he's got woes and he's got to tell them to some-one.

From *Footnotes*

HYN

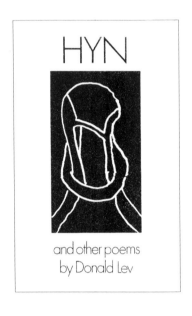

and other poems
by Donald Lev

Part One

HYN

TOTEM

This anguishing day tall with Seattle
I dream of desert beaches I have not
      seen
And walk sands cool as clouds nearest
      Heaven.

Out of the several precious driftwoods
      of Cipango
In the grey light of morning I raise a
      tabernacle
To the God Omega, gentle Lord of the
      West.

Scion of all who wait from barest dawn
(Wastrel, derelect, unatoned) for sweet
Night's reposeful mysteries – I carve
      your names,

O ancestors – in the darkness above
      my own.

FRANKIE THE MIRACLE BUM...

proclaiming his innocence
after Paul Muni in "Emile Zola"

Frankie the Miracle Bum
bringing out the sun
with a drunken song
a la Bing Crosby

Frankie the Miracle Bum
preferring Thunderbird to Gypsy Rose...
being the last word in nonconformity

Frankie the Miracle Bum
my friend for a quarter –
proclaiming his innocence,
and bringing out the sun.

HYN

Nothing spells HYN
My word HYN maybe HYNgleberry or
        HYNsorial
HYN spells nothing, begins nothing
        possible unto Webster... it is
        my very
very own HYN.
HYN in the teeth of the wind, and in
        the faces of governments and men:
HYN!

HYN uninvited, HYN unexcited, HYN
        retiring into his own HYNhood.
I built a wooden HYN once and fooled
        no one – I painted HYN in oils
and ran out of canvas – but I shall
        follow wherever
HYN lead
till HYN
vanish into darkness.

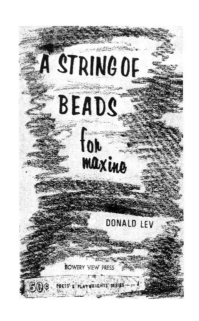

A STRING OF

BEADS

for

maxine

DONALD LEV

BOWERY VIEW PRESS

50¢ POETS' & PLAYWRIGHTS' SERIES

9

Part Two

A STRING OF BEADS
for Maxine

A STRING OF BEADS FOR MAXINE

1

NO BOND THAT IS INVISIBLE IS WEAK
NO BODY WEARS
EMPEROR'S CLOTHES
THAT IS NOT SURE
IN THE GRAND PROCESSIONAL
OF ALL HIS EMPIRE
THE CHILD'S EYE, TO BE SURE, SEES TRUE
AND EMPEROR, AND RASCAL, AND FOOL
SEE TRUE
AS COURTING BIRDS OF PARADISE

2

IT REQUIRES CONCENTRATION TO
BRING FIRES IN AND ABOVE TOGETHER
BROTHER URGENCIES REUNITED
IN ONE URGENT FLAME
FRIDAY EVENING'S KINDLING FOR THE SABBATH
IT REQUIRES CONCENTRATION TO
RECONCILE DAY WITH NIGHT – TO BEAR DARKNESS TO
            LIGHT

3

JUST BENEATH THE SURFACE OF
A SUDDEN PALE BRIEF
PAUSE IN THE HEAT OF THINGS – A GEAR MISSED – A
SHUDDERING IN THE
DAY'S CONTENT
THERE LIES A SUBSTANCE IMMEASUREABLE AS A LEAP TO
            DEATH
TO A MOBBED SIDEWALK, A POPULOUS SEA, AN END
            WE KNOW NOT OF

4

YOU POINT YOUR TOE TOWARD TREASURE
KICK THE GREAT MOON BALL IN THE AIR
BEFORE THE WHISTLE BLOWS FOUL AND THE PLAY
HAS TO CEASE AND REFORM
WHAT IS IT YOU ALWAYS DO WRONG, WHAT INFRAC-
TION
IS SO IRRESISTIBLE
IN THE GREAT TOME OF UNCOUNTABLE RULES?

5

HERE, TAKE YOUR ESSENCE
BY THE THIMBLEFUL
AND DRINK IT DOWN
A ROUND
OF ONE'S REALITY
SET IT DOWN
BY POOLSIDE, BOULEVARD, BEACHSIDE
THE LANDLOCKED HAVE COME SHOREWARD   FOR
THE
            BATHING
THEY GATHER IN CAFES   THEY SPEAK
NO MORE OF DAYS
THAN DO THE ANGELS

6

IT IS REPORTED THAT
IN CLOSED PLACES CREVICES AND CAVES
FREE BORN MYSTICS MEET
TO REPEAT IN SECRET
ALL THE REVELATIONS OF BYGONE DAYS
AND ALL THE MANIFESTATIONS OF PROPHECIES
THAT WERE TIDED IN THE GROANS OF SLAVES
WHOSE CHILDREN, THESE?

7

IT. YOU, PER-
TINENT BERRY, GOAT, TEST
BECAUSE I OVERCOME THE WORLD IN
MONUMENT.
IN LOVE IN TREMBLING IN THE FREEDOM
TO SHRIVEL TO THE WIND
TO BECOME
A THING
LESS THAN DEAD.
YOU,
I,
OVERCOME THE WORLD
BECOMING, HOWEVER SLOWLY, ALIVE

8

IS IT MERELY A CHOICE BETWEEN TWO
DEATHS? BETWEEN TWO
CLOSETS IN AN
UNBROKEN VACUUM
THEN TRULY
THE GREAT YOU IN THE MORNING OF LIFE
HAD BETTER NOT HAVE
RISEN FROM THE LONG GRASSY SLEEP IN UNBROKEN
           RIBCAGE
BUT YOU DID WAKE. AND YOU DID TASTE.

9

HANDS GRAB WRING DROP   HANDS LIFT HOLD CARRY
HANDS AVENGE   HANDS REWARD   HANDS INFLICT
           HANDS SUCCOUR
HANDS BRUTALIZE   HANDS CARESS
LET THESE HANDS OF OURS
BE WISE
AMID ALL EARTH'S POSSIBILITIES
IN CHOOSING GEMS OF LOVE AND LIFE
FROM THEIR REFUSE OF ALTERNATIVES

10

NOBLE AS RELICS OF IMPERIAL POWERS
IN THE HANDS OF DEVOUT PEASANTRY   (ONE
ANCIENT WIDOW WORE A RING
OLD, MYSTERIOUS   FOLK SOUGHT HER WISDOM
                       HER FINE FINGERS AND THE
FLASHING RING   DID NOT DESERT THEM
THIS MAJESTY I FEEL SOMETIMES...

11

THE RIGOR BROUGHT
ON CERTAIN
TENSIONS WHICH
OH IN WIND OR
OTHER SEA OF
THOUSAND NATURAL FRICTIONTHINGS
REVERBERATED, SOUNDING
BEAUTIFUL
AEOLIAN , INVOLUNTARY , ANGELIC
PURE , INTELLECT , ESSENCE
THE RIGOR   BROUGHT ON   CERTAIN

12

TOY SOLDIER MADE OF
METAL AND ENAMELED
IN MY HANDS RUBBED RUBBED HARD AND THOROUGHLY
                INTO THE EARTH
TILL IT BECAME WEATHERED AS MY HEART WAS TO BE
TOY DOLL I SUPPOSE TUCKED EVER SO TENDERLY
INTO TOY CRIB –
TENDERLY, AS YOUR HEART'S MEANT TO BE

14

TREE FOREVER SPREAD
ROOT AND BRANCH OVER ALL THE GROUND   NOT ONE
                SPOT
UNSHADED
OR LEFT UNGNARLED BY ROOT , OR IMPERVIOUS
TO LAUGHING RAIN
AND EARTHWORMS PLAY GAMES , AND MOSSES MEDITATE ,
              AND DREAMY FERNS
CATCH RAINDROPS LIKE TEARS
TO WATER GLOOMY MUSHROOMS WITH

HUNG ON FOR DEAR LIFE   THEN
DROPPED
LIKE DROPS
OFF
ICICLES
THIS IS THE FULLNESS OF
SAD OCEANS
FULL OF BEAUTY , BEAUTY , BEAUTY
THIS IS THE BREATH , IN , OUT   THE HEARTBEAT ,
             BEAT , BEAT
AND THE SWALLOW   AND THE HURT   AND THE
             HEART
THIS IS THE ETERNAL TERRESTRIAL

15

TO REPEAT   TO REVIEW   TO RECEIVE
FROM FRAGMENTS PAST PRESENT FUTURE
THE WHOLE MESSAGE
YOUR
FACE OR VOICE
WHEN EITHER LIGHTS SUDDENLY HOWEVER BRIEFLY
FLICKERS LIGHT OF
SUNS THROUGHOUT THE COSMOS
AND I KNOW
AND WOULD HAVE YOU KNOW
HAPPINESS IS POSSIBLE

16

OUT THERE   WHERE YOUNG STARS   BENT ON EONS
                OF DESTRUCTION
BURN NEVER   AND EVER
WHERE THE POLES OF
ALL PLANETS CONJOIN
WITH IMPOSSIBLE ANGELS
WHERE HEARTS OF ALL
FLESH , OF STATUES AND SWALLOWS
COME TOGETHER AS
TWIN FIGURES
TWELVE , OR ELEVEN :   MY PEN

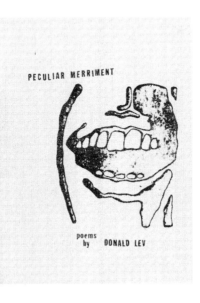

PECULIAR MERRIMENT

poems
by DONALD LEV

Part Three

Peculiar Merriment

THE FUNERAL

pallbearers, seven of them
loitered on the steps of
the great granite mausoleum
i was one of them
i'd a bag of marbles in my left hand pocket
and i
nervously listened to the
ticking of my wristwatch
the corpse arrived just in time for burial
he had a clean suit on, but
his shoes were filthy
we remembered it had been raining and the cemetery
    roads were unpaved, so we forgave him
he asked for a few minutes alone with his wife, which
    we granted
the rabbi began fumbling with his prayer book, the
undertaker was getting neurotic about
too many creases in the
american flag
the troop of boy scouts began playing an impromptu
    game of tag
y'know, i thought, this could go on forever, so i stopped.

SANCTUS

veil after veil dropped
from the bosom of the beloved
incense burned higher and higher
my inner man
(him in whom spirit was beauty)
climbed my throat like a cry from nethermost hell
"ecstacy"
some scholar muttered, chewing on an orange peel

THE TRAGIC LIFE OF BEE BRUMBLE

hive-free the bee
buzzes for sport
short
his life , he says
why not buzz where he
please
so buzzes him
into deserts
out of blooming season
thorny and
unfragrant
the desert is then
and nobody but himself
to blame, save maybe
a negligent queen
and a touch of insanity

.

FRAGMENT OF A LETTER TO ONE'S HOME PLANET

operating under the
influences
of the
abbot of the
solar system
, that is Father Sunspot
i have been entering ever more deeply into an
anti-scientific phase
of practical sanctity
where everything is a drag

MIRACLE

you rose three
feet off the ground
just now
you thought i
wasn't watching, and i
wasn't i
just happened to have turned around
and i wish i hadn't
you've complicated my life with your prank
and if i
regard you from now on
with deliberate disbelief,
you have yourself to thank.

CONTE (for Balzac, my tormenting spirit)

ronel, First name claude
was duly registered in the baptismal records of the village of
C--- on the third day of august, 1796
he was three days old
he died
one hundred and
ninety nine years later
cursing God.

NOCTURNE

Trees where you thought the night through
grew gnarled and barren against one moon
for your thoughts were winter, and older than a glacier
and the robin froze in his denuded nest
and the only the wisest owl, who took it as a jest
knew it was spring, and in his poor voice, sang

HIEROGLYPHS

hieroglyphs mounting slanting tombwall
i am reading them
they are quite ancient
they speak of death
they speak of life also , but with
some embarrassment
they speak of the death of the sungod
they speak little of the
earth ship that sailed his
ashes to the sun

HIGGINS AGAIN

higgins again
why?
Pat Higgins was an old man, use to be
an elevator operator at the
Forest Hills Inn
and used to sit in
Marshall's Bar night after night till closing time
drinking beer and stout and
talking to himself
he fell off his stool a
couple of times
before he died
Why
night after night do I
attempt this poem?

SARDINE

net began falling
from
nowhere
that's
all i
can
tell you
i
think i
was or
seemed to myself to
have been a
solitary creature
before then

TRANSMIGRATION

heat wouldn't let up
god! i
stripped naked tried
to get
under something or
over something or
just away
space
it was
that kind of
heat which is
space's opposite
then i
just sat and boiled
and then some clod
dipped me
bit by bit in butter
and ate me
lately
my lives have moved in other circles
who can blame me

SHAGGY GHOST STORY
(somewhat after the fiction of H. P. Lovecraft)

how it ever came about
that we should fix upon this
desolate region to make our abode, and
in this cold house, this stilted hovel
to attempt our dwelling perplexes me to this day

gwendolyn was always one to move about
and now focused her scattered cravings upon the countryside
we drove north instead of south turned right instead of left
and found ourselves in this place

we took it. we didn't like it, but we took it.
the price was not high, nor was it low.
the house was moderately decrepit, but in fair repair,
but nothing was there to really recommend it. but we took it.

the first night we spent here, the lights blew out.
the next evening the water gave out.
the third, the wind howled, the fourth the

thing

appeared

in the corridor

gwendolyn drove back to the city, and i remained
to investigate whatever it was, but it never came back again

31

LUTHERAN VESPERS

moving
silence
stirring above
candlelight
Bach
to northern arches
slender
as the
woman beside me
as the hymnal
between her palms

GENESIS

Sunward glaring
Grew a garden
Topping Heaven
Uprooting Hell

An angel fell
Crushing stems
Flattening blooms
Spreading Heaven

The hand of Mammon
Thrusted upward
Roots destroying
Lifted Hell

The human swell
Possessed the plain
A hapless flood
At home in deserts

REQUIEM FOR AN OIL TYCOON

untimely end
he was only
seventy three and had
so much left to do
he
felt a
challenge
in the future
raised hell to
meet it
advised two or three presidents to do likewise
some people ignored him completely
they didn't count
he counted
he counted a lot
he counted night and day
he counted his pennies
till they became dollars
he counted his
dollars till they became millions
he counted you and me like the hairs on his head
this strange god

CREATION MYTH

naturally, the whole plan was a flop
they just didn't see things from every angle before they
began, like
you and i would have
the whole business is
lying in a
heap right over there
where those phoenixes are nesting

Introduction by William Packard

Part Four

Intercourse With the Dead

ON THE DEATH OF A YOUNG POET (for Adrian)

he was a young god dying in a
rosy vision
he was the god of chance, and
under all his innocence
was a ghastly schemer
water nymphs combed him
out of their sea green hair
the king of the deep cleansed him
from his yellow stare
the whole earth groaned
under his shortness of years
i knew him briefly, he
seemed a nice, gentle
young man

THE VISITORS

joyously the parson received the three strangers
the old fellow probably thought it was one of those
visitation things like in the bible
and couldn't do enough for them to make them
          comfortable
before they had been there one hour they had him tie
his wife and children to their beds and gag their mouths
then had him cordially help them to all funds on hand
on the way out they blessed him.
they really blessed him, for
in fact they were visiting angels
carrying out part of some very wide sweeping plan.

THE BRAIN WITH THE ORANGE TAG

could you hand me
that brain
with the orange tag? thanks.
yes, i think this'll do fine.
its thoughts are so
deep, bright, and sincere...

THE WILDERNESS

god stopped for gas at
a little esso station somewhere in nevada
(those were the days when he drove the earth anonymously)
"fillerup" says he in his anonymous voice, and
if you don't mind, please check the oil and water
everything's right up full, says the wizened old attendant
who was too courteous to let on
that he knew Whose car he serviced
god kept right on going at a goodly pace
for he wanted to make it to San Francisco before daybreak.
he made it, but
got arrested on the freeway for
speeding and driving with an expired license
he was thrown in jail and has never really been heard from since
i only tell you this
because i
used to be a prophet
before my license expired
i let it run out because i got tired
of living in motels
and always being treated so damned politely.

THE CIRCUS

pitted against the first lion
was the gladiator Nicholas
master of the hammer
he broke two of the beast's fangs before he was torn apart
next was a slender girl named April
who tried charming her lion
out of his wits, and almost succeeded
she was followed by forty young christians, pacifist and
vegetarian to a man
but by that time most of the crowd had gone home

MUSIC AND POETRY

orpheus broke a string on his lyre
he went down to the music store to
buy a replacement
i went with him
because i liked him, or
i liked the odor
in a music store
or
because i had nothing better to do
i thought of taking lyre lessons one time
but gave it up
i wasn't orpheus
i was silenus
i never went to hell for anyone, but i have my songs to sing
        just the same

later that evening we both got drunk, the kid and i
i guess i got drunker. i
remember trying to
well, advise him, never
look back, i said, never
look back
he just laughed, and
left me for the drunken old sot i am...
next time i seen him, he was a broken man...

PADDLING AN OLD CAMUS (WITH YOU)

Said She sadly: I lost my purpose in a crowded laundromat in Algiers. The sky was so clear and blue, and the sand so white. I couldn't see what I was doing. So I ordered an extra dessert that night and retired early.

Said He: I watched you as you crossed from the laundromat to the beach, but did not follow you... You looked so wonderfully solitary, I pictured you among the dunes and gulls. I returned to the hotel and waited. You came and sat down. I did not join you. I had other matters to attend to.

And did you attend to them?

Of course.

To your satisfaction?

It was a favor, for a friend.

To your friend's satisfaction then?

I do not know. I shall never know. I am never again to see my friend.

Why is this?

He is dead.

Dead?

I killed him.

Killed him? you...?

That was the favor.

I suppose he is satisfied then.

Who knows?

I lost my purpose...
I know.

How do you know?

You dropped it in the street on the way to the beach. I picked it up.

Oh? You will return it to me then?

No.

No?

I... sold it.

Sold it?

I needed money.

I see.

Let's walk on the beach.

Why?

Why not.

Shall we always love each other?

Why do you ask?

A woman asks these things.

Oh.

Well?

You want an answer.

Of course.

I have no answers.

I have no purpose.

Shall we walk on the beach?

Why not?

SCENARIO

relying on his
memory for faces
the classic detective hacked through the plastic jungle
in search of the elusive king linoleum
all warnings ignored, including those of
the nameless headless clay pigeon
he continued his incongruous pursuit
through blood and headlights and dynamite
once three wax goons in white
accosted him with rubber knives
he melted them in one thirsty bite!
then the chick in the transparent sarong
tried blinding him with acid
he left her in the cold moonlight, the hound of heaven
licking her slight smile...
there was something so wild in his shallow scowl
you had to like him...

DEFINITION

Half the amount necessary to
sustain it
was poured into the
slowly materializing spirit glass
i held hands with
a dentist on my right and an
awol sister of charity on my left
then came rapping, syncopated rapraprapping
then came the jumble of voices
and i was
at the beginning
then came one single voice out of the glass
it was my voice and it sounded as if i were drowning
after we'd all taken a sip from the glass
a light was turned on inside it

POEM TO BREAK IN A NEW SET OF DENTURES WITH

gesture capsized.
the magnificent imposter
drowning
in his own incompletion
A russian mathematician named melvin smerdlin
discovered
the only rule applicable to
any kind of distortion
$x=x/y$
his explanation
has never been understood by anyone anywhere, yet
fame came to him
along with a drawerful of new underwear
compliments of the soviet academy
the weather presently may be said to be stormy, a
poor day for canoeing
but a good day for biting and chewing

POEM FOR A NEW YEAR

i eat
an onion every morning
then i milk the cows
the sun comes up so liquid sometimes
you can hear it like a little silver bell

VACATION

it did seem
as if we had lost our way
amid the winding streets and the chalk white buildings
of the silent city
but it was a holiday
the cobalt skies the
warm south breeze the
cerulean blue bay under our touring eyes
we might have been slides
we were!

PROPHECY

by astronomical projection
man should reach perfection
by the year three thousand and five
with a conservative Republican in the White House, and
the Pope working out of a storefront in South Brooklyn
a computer named Rudy should work out the rest
on the basis of all conceivable data

MIRACLE PLAY

drooping over
a long rope stretched across the room for
just this purpose,
charlie the
parisian
took his forty winks
purple eggs
danced in crimson yolks
while bagpipers from the pyrenees played jigs and reels in his
        hopscotch sleep
he woke to a dawn of roasted oats
a taystee breadtruck splashed him as he crossed the street
for his eyeopener
a day unfolded its adventures
as grim as a game of hide and go seek
have you heard of Everyman, says charlie to
a two second old pal
i am he
all the world knows it

SPIRITUAL

jordan river rose two feet, drowned
the prophet macabel
who'd stretched out on the sand to take some sun
and mull over his latest premonition...

THERE IS
STILL TIME

THE POETRY OF
DONALD LEV

Part Five

There Is Still Time

THERE IS STILL TIME

god is crawling on his hands and knees, so to speak,
looking for the key to turn the whole thing off.
he dropped it in one of the streets of glory and it
fell thru a grating into the depths of perdition.
he is trying to get it up with a gummed stick, it
isn't easy, and it is most trying to his
       infinite patience.

PSALM

how do you
upend
the great stone jug of ink
that sits on horeb
ready to recreate the word
in all its savage power
without a blotter?
the nerve!
the world is my rorschach. i
shall not want for revelation.

JUST ONCE

Just once, when I was quite small, did anything happen at all. Not that i recall
anything of importance (well i know now
I was too young at first, and then too old).
Over and over elders repeated
inchoate remembrance from blank edges
of my own suppressed life's pseudo-pages.
Known and unknowing, infancy stretches.
Then knowing and unknown, march step changes.
"Order in the court," the judge of the quick
and the dead parts the sea with his gavel.
As I start across, he rescinds his order,
and I am stranded on the embankment. When
the suspension bridge is built it is too late.

THE PASSENGER

a child in a superman costume
is teetering on the edge of a brooklyn roof
as the elevated m train i'm on passes by.
i mutter in passing,
        "don't try…"

AUGUST POEM WRITTEN IN FEBRUARY

just a minute.
what's snow doing on your shoes in august.
august is the cruelest month, when
the sun comes down
and you have snow on your shoes.
august is the month of sunrise and sunset
over cemeteries and crematoria.
august is an apple too large to eat.
and if you have snow on your shoes in august,
        you will stand accused!

HOW IT FEELS TO BE MORTAL

Under blankets of dreams, mummy wrappings
twined with pieces of tissue, broken shoe-
laces, promises of eternal life.
My place in the world – where is it? My flesh,
what is or was it? These aren't my eyes!
Then feel...(as they say, "Once more, with feeling")!
Taste the dust of eternity. Listen.
Maybe you can hear your next breath coming.
Grant an interview. Hold a press conference.
Tell the world how it feels to be mortal,
how true riches only wait interment.
God looks out an elevated train window
passing a cemetery in the rain. He
cannot follow the kaddish we try to say.

THE REPUBLIC

opposite the
tower from which
lookouts used to
search out enemies, is the wall against which
potential disrupters of the social order were shot.

did you see the last such exhibition?
i was one of the marksmen.
A wonderful cloud dipped low out of heaven to
        shade our eyes
a slight breeze wafted in from the ocean.
all was peaceful.
the seven terrorists, there was one woman
        among them,
were silent and orderly and ultimately
        cooperative.

i am glad all that is over now.
after those seven were executed the state became
        quite secure.
we had nothing to do but sit on the rocks and
        clean our weapons.
one day, while cleaning his weapon, one of our men
        accidentally shot the lookout.
we are waiting now, by the wall.

THE TERROR

The terror struck
before daybreak
our neighbors in sheets,
our servants with pitchforks,
our baker, our barber, our banker
all bearing torches,
surrounded our
apartment
our landlord refused to send up heat
some nut in a jet plane tried pelting us with bricks
the mayor told a gathering in queens that he was
       preparing to pass laws against us
the police just stood around and watched
the fire department took its time
an ambulance dispatched from mount sinai
       got lost in central park
one poet called it all a cosmic joke.

ROUTINE DECISION

if you disagree with the verdict, the judge
      warned the firing squad,
you might circulate a petition. of course your
      standing would be doubtful,
and you would certainly be accused of conflict
      of interest.

the leader of the squad, one sergeant aimes,
      saluted thoughtfully, then
marched his men out to the courtyard
      in double file, pushing the
prisoner along on his wheeled coffin between them.

the execution was carried out routinely.
      After which a vote was taken
by the nine squad members, who voted five to
      four against circulating
the petition.

SADAT

ultimately
it is better to sit down to an overly
cholesterolized breakfast
at the market diner, than
to be three hours dead, shot
off a reviewing stand
from a parade of one's own loyal armed forces.
(at seven am, 2 hours late, i am getting dressed
        in Brooklyn,
preparing for a day of cab driving. He is
        standing, in the cairo
afternoon, in full uniform, preparing
        for the grave)
Anwar, peacemaker, born on christmas day,
        under the sign of the goat.

MIDEAST REPORT

rioting occultists
threw spells at police
in the Israeli capital today
as the Begin government issued its proclamation
separating the west bank from the jordan river.
the ghost of harry houdini spoke for five hours;
  the
grand mufti for three.
Larry Meanstreak of the American Indian Movement
was also on hand to denounce Zionism in the
  u.s. cavalry.

JERICHO

jericho was an unforgettable sight, as the
mists parted and we entered the surrounding vale.
it was the first city some of us had ever seen!
i felt like wailing! someone handed me a horn.
i blew my heart out. then someone
must have dropped a brick on me.

(perhaps Pierre who lives next door to me
        in Paris and hates my guts) no
that explains not my life in Jericho,
        not necessarily.
when i came to, the walls were down
        but there was this
incredible hostility, like Pierre,
        who i suspect is
anti-semitic.

A PAGE FROM MY DIARY
(IF I HAD ONE)

friday
i woke up too early
i put on my
blackest cloak and my
bleakest stare
and strode forth to my
gig uptown
i
played folk oboe
in a progressive
bluegrass band
we played at yankee
stadium between seasons.
i loved the morning drizzle and the
morning
i am president
of the mourner's club
we meet
at a different cemetery
each weekend
we mourn everything

CITY LIFE

He eyed my hidden hand. Distrust
shone under his eyelids like two
nightlights. My public fingers drew
back into fist. My other hand
remained hidden. A line started
forming behind me. Another
formed behind him. The clerk slept on
in her booth. The sky clouded up.
Thunder was heard. A drop of rain
fell on my nose. My public fist
twitched. The other hand moved in my
coat pocket. My enemy's heart
jumped out of his throat and landed
at my feet. I picked it up and
handed it back to him. Tension
eased and the lines started to move.

MY WINE

soc
rates
raised
his cup
up
nervously
and toasted
the rising sun
then
drained
the cosmos
of its poison
though you and i
refill it many times,
and leave it
within reach of small children

THE DRY SPELL

late night:
perhaps
a willow below this window
has something to say
that the moon has not thought of.
i have nothing to say.
the books i have been reading have nothing to say.
the miracle reported in the newspapers yesterday
(the statue that knelt, picked up a flower at her feet, and
returned to her pedestal) even that
had nothing to add to anyone's knowledge
i have thought of going far away, to
casablanca perhaps or
cartagena
but
where would i be
upon debarkation.
nowhere that interesting
unless i tied my shoelaces together by mistake, fell
between shore and ship's deck got
rescued by mermaids and set
to dry upon the cyclops' isle
then i might have an interesting story to tell you.
but i doubt it.

SIXTEENTH POEM OF LOVE

god! i love the woman fashioned from my
cracked rib
growing out like tea
she is very leafy, tree like
, a garden of verity
how long i was asleep during her making!

longer than she was during mine.

FOR GOD'S SAKE, LOOK!

i put my
coat
over my head, my
hat floated
a few inches above that, so
it appeared to
the casual observer that
i was without a head,
which is ridiculous.
my head being where
my heart beat,
under my coat.

WEDDING IN WESTCHESTER

my friend homer led me to a place
where they were barbecueing whole sheep
we tore off handfuls of sizzling fat
and ate to our hearts' content.
all homer's family was there,
mine too.
and homer's old mother,
and mine, too.
a young girl was being married.
her grandmother caught her bouquet.

SOLILOQUY

I am very sad and very unexcited.
The Creator forged me like a signature
upon a worthless check.
I lie around uncashable.
The rain has already blurred my ink.
The sun has yellowed my paper.
Hoo boy, am i sick!

MASHED POTATO IN MY BEARD

here, harry, have
some mashed potato.

i wondered why she called me
harry. (mostly she
calls me hugh.)

thanks said i, i'm on a diet.

"you're a liar" she whispered menacingly.
then she
pushed the bowl into my face.

which is why you see
mashed potato in my beard.

i just wonder why she called me harry.

FALL AND WINTER
(A RUSSIAN NOVEL)

zetzov was only thirty versts from
putzov, but i refused to walk.
anatoly! i implore you to drive me
to zetzov. i'll give you four
rubles.
anatoly spit contemptuously. "six"
he replied.
but i only have four. for the love of
God, anatoly!
he signaled me to climb up into the
wagon beside him.
when i reached the house in retznikoyaslav alley
grechunka was away in the forest feeding her wolves.
or so nikolai, her father's half-brother and her slave,
would have led me to believe.

but i did not believe,   i could not believe!

so i set forth for the quarter called svetlaya,
a haven for gypsies pimps and poles,
searching for my grechunka, to repay
her the thirty rubles i had cheated
out of her worthless uncle prince pitkin.
but she was nowhere about.

let her feed her wolves! i shouted,
and ordered more vodka

my head was spinning as they led me away.

SEDER

macedonian was spoken at this one.
why i will never know.
in brighton beach i thought all jews were pure thracian.
the void
compelling me to go forward
closed behind me. i was thrust naked
into a day different from all days.
i was not confused.
i refused to be.

JULYAD

july, month of julius caesar, had
come and gone for the fortyeighth time for me.
vanity of vanities, my generation passeth away.
just the other day
a fly drowned in my cup of tea,
leaving no dependents as far as i could see.

WISDOM POEM

The years go round like rising and
falling horses. My eyes see less
of what they look at, but my mind's
cluttered with better examples.

Overnight I have become what
yesterday has prepared me for.

END OF YEAR KVETCH
(*for Richard, who's beyond this now*)

cliffs of broken rock, me
stumbling over them, my
feet cut and bleeding, the shattered
tablets of my
destined work

no forget it
it is a cold night
on a windy corner

i stand with tall bagged can of beer
awaiting destiny

i have work running errands for several devils
who pay me
what i'm worth
there are no benefits

but i find an old portable
typewriter abandoned in a vacant lot
it types poorly but it types
i use yesterday's newspaper to type on

the work goes
not well
but on

THE PESSIMIST WAITS FOR DAWN

ok it was only
a little light
that refused to be turned on
the switch was broken
not a big deal
but it was dark
the night would end and
supposedly there would be sunlight to see by
and a new switch could be purchased and installed
so why am i sitting in darkness so desolate?

TRADITION

let me introduce myself in case you do not already know
me.
i am your father.
it was i who deposited you in that itchy straw.
it was i who refused to let you cut your hair until you were
14.

it was i who hid in the shadows your whole life.
it is i who demand everything from you now.

you are at attention, facing the sun.
i am the sun.

your blindness is my desire.

BEFORE ALL THIS MESS

Before all this mess was a time of un-
complicated promiscuity when
the lips were rounder, the ears wider, and
the eyes cleaner. We hopped over rocks and
urinated in tall grasses. We were
glad to find water and wise in our search
for meat. We gambled only for pleasure
and wrote books of five thousand characters

GENIUS

later
that night
the moon began falling
i cried "watch out!"
everybody was going his own way
what was i to do but
stand under it

this moon we know is not the first to fall,
        nor will it be the last.
there is still time to sort out the future from the past.
there is time to choose.
to be or not to be one
who stands under the falling moon.

THE DAYS OF THE EASTER BUNNY

DONALD LEV

Part Six

The Days of the Easter Bunny

THE DAYS OF THE EASTER BUNNY

lying in wait for any prey at all,
oddly drawn and under played you can't have everything
    at once, but one thing at a time
all
forgotten this time is the rule – the first rule of the sea.
to hide. over the rest of the season.
one finger at a time.

go tell it on the mountain, tell it in the restrooms, tell it
in the funeral homes
and speak of it as thou walkest over the outstretched
    legs of the dying.
that the king of darkness has arisen this
otherwise bright afternoon
and he demands his cup of tea with no apology
Who is the king of darkness? he that hath long black
    fingernails and weareth many
wristwatches which he tries to sell at the crossroads
we shall bow to him at sunrise and again at sunset, but
    to no avail.

i have wasted enough time with this music. you can't
    dance to it, you can only listen to it
and nod your head dumbly and walk out into
wet loud streets and try in vain to hail a taxi and
    wind up with the phantom gypsy who
takes you uptown by the crook of your arm and you
    fall asleep completely dissipated and
comes the dawn it starts again and you run a mile and
    feel your pulse run faster than you
and you shower shave shine and dress and confront
    your world at your best
and you'll know no rest
yet weariness will not be allowed
in the terrible kingdom the crucified was crucified for
    over and over till it sank in

old shirts and socks in a drawer, a window open four
    fingers too dirty to see out the
panes. a sticky sarsparilla bottle and last thursday's

times folded to the business section

i am in a trance, sir i'll be right with you

do you want something from the bar?

Justice? on the rocks or straight up?

joy of bellringing, encircling spring
the lilies leaping over hearts clearing for the blast
baseball season nearing, you know, smug yankees in
    pinstripes looking for the perfect pitch

demonstrably erogenous, the flesh of roses about
    the house, thorns sticking the flesh at
all exits and entrances
we have returned to the soil to lie around among
    sacks of potatoes
all the while a late snow flurry falls slowly and
    church bells sound
and great trumpet lilies played by country angels tickle
    the eardrums and make the noses
twitch and the potato eyes smart with teardrops

hallelujah! we are risen.

we are haled before the judge and fined $45 plus a
    surcharge of $15 and told to leave town
yet i personally feel rich
having ceased upon the midnight with no pain and
    risen in the dawn with just a little pain
while
the ayatollah the rabbi and the cardinal archbishop
    call forth their cries abroad with such
ecstacy

i trod i trod i trod bearing one potato at a time
to market to market to market
and i will turn my produce over
and gain the whole world
and i will place my eggs in many baskets
my portfolio will be regularly reviewed by the best – by

ivan boesky himself
and i shall fear no evil

new years arrive like good quarterly reviews, about twice a
    year, once for the jews once for the common era
between is spring
with my annual spring haircut, medium, not too short,
    there may be cold weather yet
i tell the russian barber who is arguing in yiddish with
    someone behind us
as his radio blows rocknroll a new love
he was still playing nostalgic old russian torch songs on
    cassettes my last visit only last
september and so the seasons melt away in universal
    american slush
and reagan is not subpoenaed to witness for true north,
    thank god how could they have
thought to do such a thing to an ex-president
score another victory for the return of divine right,
    happy easter, hallelujah!
however, my children
who are reading these tattered pages in your little holes
    in some future when
i am truly appreciated,
i know i have wasted our time with too much
topicality, so vague now in your
century like jesus walking on water or bobby sands'
    fasting to death
or the rosenbergs' ceremonial burning moments
    before Sabbath

let us bow the head reverently, if you
have forgotten how i shall include directions, meanwhile
    you may salute the flag i'm sure
reagan's posterity wouldn't let you forget that!
rise now and leave
your holes, leave my tattered pages behind for the
    librarians to pick up and sort out
while we go strolling through the woods hunting
    for microfiche

i change direction excuse the suddenness

i am back in spring of 1989 i am back at the very moment
    of daylight saving time's
restoration hallelujah the
bunny already surfeited on turnips and radishes dances
    in the screaming garden and i
awake screaming to discover i have only lost one hour
    of my life
which shall be returned, perfected in the fall
hallelujah!
on the outskirts of nineveh, a dwarf looks up over a high
    bench and sees snow white and her
step mother prancing along the sidewalk toting shopping
    bags from bonwit teller chattering
away like life long girl friends, the dwarf wipes away a tear
    of joy and gets back to work
whistling a happy tune, hallelujah!
is it true once you get to be president you can get away
    with anything?

down the treasuries of the years a small silver steamroller
    reduces glory to tinsel
i think i shall
stop and have another drink and try to rethink the whole
process as i know and have known it

i think i should learn to treasure my regrets, perhaps to
    earn them a place among future
antiques
i feel green
that is not a good feeling
it is not necessarily a bad feeling
it may not be a feeling at all
i am trying to write intimate poetry, but in a grand epic
    style i am trying to impress
my audiences and press upon their brows
crowns of thorny nudgings

so whistle a happy tune, let the lily bugles blow
let the easter bunny hop on your lap and get you to
    order champagne! hallelujah!

TWENTIETH CENTURY LIMITED

by
DONALD LEV

Part Seven

Twentieth Century Limited

TWENTIETH CENTURY LIMITED
*(which is the name of a train and is the name
of this poem)*

Vest pockets thumbed, time pieces examined,
ready to fly at a moments notice,
we carried our own decks of cards, were shrewd
to the point of no return. Fearing fear
itself, we plunged blithely into the tunnel of nightmare
where terror winks at terror.

I USED TO BE IN THE CIGAR BUSINESS

The ash end of the cigar brightened
my life. It was light and substance and
truth. I knelt before the end of the
cigar. I wept over it as I
thought of Havana, as I thought of
Jerusalem and Kiev and Man-
hattan. I tried to maintain an en-
viable position in the business
community all the while
but my ash worship was getting the
better of me. Friends started avoid-
ing me. Enemies began praising me,
taking me out for long lunches
in obscure delicatessens – feasts
of liverwurst and limburger. I
couldn't tell what they were up to, but I
kept my eyes on their cigars, watching
and waiting for the ashes to fall...

LIVING WITH INFINITY
(for Enid Dame)

1.
goose feathers fluttering on stale air –
cigar smoke layered above the feathers,
hymns pouring forth from a radio tuned
to the family gospel hour, jesus himself
disguised as the statue of liberty
walking alongside an ark shaped (the more one's
mirror eye unblurs) like an mx missile.

2.
what of the race for the deep cup of mead
swallowed in one gulp by a victor
too anxious to get to the next contest?

3.
their third day at sea may have been the worst.
two days from land yet no one accepting
the perhaps infinity of ocean...

4.
noah stalking the deck nervously,
his sons awkward and watchful in their waiting.

5.
my father said, "lower your head when walking
under anything."   I've never forgotten
to honor my father with bowed head.

OPORTO

Oporto is a summer festival
around its famous beaneries, especially
where are served the famous Oporto bean
which is like a jelly bean, only firmer.
On August 14th, and lasting 8 days until August 22nd
is the famous Oporto Bean Festival
where all the beautiful people of Oporto
dress up like beans
and do the colorful
bean dance which is the most sensuous
dance imaginable.
On the Friday preceding August 14th
all the Oporto folk, known as
Oportunistas, bring their
first bean offerings to the
Cathedral that stands overlooking
the Oporto Baths
where Christopher Columbus used to go
to wash up
and get straight.
The Baths are now the property of
Helmsley International Hotels and Motels
and it costs the touristas a pretty penny to
clean up in them.
Oporto is the seventh largest city in Europe
and has the fourth lowest suicide rate.

BRITAIN

Hole in one!
The regiment applauded.
The pheasants rose from their nests and circled the field.
It was a great day for riding.
General Eisenhower waded on shore. He'd forgotten
  his tote bag.
The battle still raged in the passionate blue skies,
but the first robin was early.
Legend has it when this occurs
the reddleman sleeps four centuries.
Aaron the Jew, looking wily under his pink fez,
begins to argue
about what time curfew begins and ends.

Lovers stroll the greensward; no telling
how long an afternoon was put in for.
The children's cloudless sport already over,
The brightest of them race towards us,
their little baskets of eggs swaying wildly.
Hip hip hooray, someone shouts.
Hip hip hooray, someone else answers.
A piper is heard parading the hill,
his solitary air descending with the sun.

THE HUMAN CONDITION IN BRIGHTON BEACH

Did you see the salt shaker?
It has been carried away.
And the onion that lay in slices on this very table only yesterday
is likewise mysteriously vanished.
And the lace curtains that moved so gracefully in that window
are gone also.
And the porcelain pitcher from Mexico, I'd never think to miss it,
but I see it's not in its usual place on the bookshelf.

What has happened to the independent clutter about me?
What tricks are occurring, and why?
There was a third left to that stick of butter only just a
moment ago.
Where is it now?

It's not madness. I am sure of that. I am sure of that.
Madness is such an oldfashioned idea and it would never
    apply to me.
My friends would have told me by now. They hold nothing
    back from me.

I think I'd better go for a walk. I'll take an umbrella.
I'll walk over to the beach to have a look at the sea,
or I'll go up to Coney Island Avenue and buy a knish.
A kasha knish, maybe, with a cup of very light coffee.
Then I'll go to the post office and buy some stamps.
Just so I can stand in line and grumble together
with everybody else and watch how the wiley Russians
sneak to the front of the line. But what did I do with my key?

This is beginning to get to me. I can't leave the house
    without my key.
And obviously, if I stay here I'll go crazy.

GLORY

you're in your glory everything's going
ok ok everything's going o –
k use this happiness well it can't be
stored lavish it throw it away it can't be
stored i hear your feet tapdancing on
the second floor photos of you are e-
verywhere life is a fifth avenue dou-
ble decker bus eternally passing
rockefeller center's christmas tree as
cherry cheeked songsters carol in the pla=
za the thrill of catching a first fish of
finally getting <u>her</u> into bed and
she trills oh i'm all wet that magical
summer of fifty six a rowboat an
island a music that is everything

A TRAGEDY

george did it
don't let him!
but he did it already
you let george do it?
well he insisted

THE NEW WORLD ORDER

1.
interlocking directorates

2.
this grid of sugar cubes

3.
an aerial view a smear on a slide

4.
on one side ants preparing for war
on the other, war's end, defying
geneva convention, eating enemies
consuming protein for the next onslaught
the social animal perfected and incorporated
with world-wide interlocking directorates

PROGRESS

large as life but no larger,
the white
raven spread its wings between shining seas and took off.

there was a burst of foul air from his exhaust
to tell the world not to just stand there

IN MOVING A STONE

sometimes in moving a stone
from one end of a field to another
a mystical purpose is hit upon
justifying the activity.

TWILIGHT

DONALD LEV

Part Eight

Twilight

TWILIGHT

Dearest. The rainbow collapsed today.
No one had been riding it thank goodness
I have negatives soaking in my darkroom
in a solution of tears and acid
that is no solution and will beget
no positives. In one of these negatives
you may be said to be silhouetted
against an empty sky. We shall see.

Don't dread anything. From point of view
of nothingness even vision farthest
back in the mind is no starting point.
Red letter days come and go to be sure.
Our transports seem to flow, but are mostly bleak
the photos show, and recede like winter.

Receding. A hair line. A shoreline.
A breathline. A heartline. My palms turn upward,
then backward to cover my eyes. It is
a gesture the meaning of which I
am uncertain. There are no thoughts behind
the covered eyes when I do this. Only
a sense like the sound of a river
entering an unquiet harbor.

Listen. You can hear laughter in the waves
as being is transformed into memory;
as when a father dies or a wise word
is recorded for posterity.

OTHER PEOPLE'S SURREALISM

geriatric advice notwithstanding, the
tall plutocrat with the white feather sprouting
from his skull came forward on his hands and knees
begging yours truly to leave him out of this
poem. "i detest other people's
surrealism," he said. "it is like
other people's feces." Love me, love my
feces, i told him, leaving him goveling...

COPING IN A FOREST OF FETA TREES

i opened up a goat's nest of troubles first of all
i mistook an honest dime for somebody else's
headaches when the new car was delivered without its
stereo i commissioned a battery of pro-
fessional crime investigators to research the
assumptions under which the terms of the agreement
were reached whether bomb threat or gunpoint inculcated
or did not implicate or even whether any
of this applied the chill factor of course had to be
considered as well as the entertainment value
my migraine began leaking and just then my brother
called from hong kong to pry into my business i told
him i was shopping for a new long distance service
he suggested at&t i told him those let-
ters made my teeth hurt and i would prefer less personal
advertising i could tell he was hurt by the
way he said goodbye forever some people can't take
a joke others can't take anything else i knew a
singer once who lost a finger in a sink full of
dishes everybody helped her look but nobody
found it if i were rich she said i could afford a
dozen fingers but at my age they don't grow on trees

THE COMEDY
(an epic poem in six cantos)

The personages of the poem are: a delivery boy for a neighborhood grocery store called the Elrose Superette. He may
be named "Dante." God, Who appears as what once would
have been termed a "cranky shut-in." Charon. An elderly,
probably homeless woman. Orson Welles, who is Dante's
guide in Hades. Souls in Hell including Edward Koch, a
poet, and John the Odd Jobs Man. Eli and Rose, propri-
etors of the Elrose Superette.
The time is the eternal present. The place is Brooklyn.

Canto I

i stand before the gates of heaven
  holding a carton full of groceries.
  i'm sent round to the back door with my burden.

It's a long way. i feel i'll never get there.
  i'd drop the carton and run, but the order's
  c.o.d.   *says who?*   "it's marked right here,

c.o.d."   *damn! i ain't paying. you can
  take your fucking groceries and go to hell...*
  "My Lord!"   *Child!* ... *oh, ok. put it down*

on that chair. i'm tired. i've gotta close my eyes.
i'll attend to it later, when i rise...

Canto II

foul smelling place ... odor of linament,
  or of decay. dust, stains, books and papers piled
  up in indiscriminate heaps. the old ... gent

must read everything. cobwebs. radiator
  hissing. Him starting to snore. i look around
  for a telephone. i have to call the store

to find out what they want me to do.
  no phone anywhere. the place gives me the creeps.
  from the darkest end of the huge cluttered room

112

that is heaven comes clatter like the sound
  of radio static turned up to the
  decibel equivalent of a thousand

new york city subway stations at rush hour.
  "the communion of saints attempting
  to communicate" is the thought that seems to pour

itself dreamlike over my mind's horizon
  as i begin boldly to penetrate
  darkness in search of the telephone.

from darkness to darkness racing with all might,
at last i come to a place of no light.

Canto III

from there to a place of little light is
  but a step and i take it. the static
  gradually subsides and my senses

begin returning. i behold a spectre
  who in all probability is in charge,
  puffing a cigar behind a tall counter.

i ask if there's a phone on the premises.
  he points his wet cigar over my shoulder.
  "can't ya see? across da street," he wheezes.

i cross the dim lighted street thru mists
  that rise from the dead who alone know brooklyn
  to find the only pay phone on the fritz.

lost, cut off, bereft of hope and aimless,
i wander in hell. a chilly place!

Canto IV

forlornly i walk the long boring
  avenue of stores gated up – it must
  be sunday, or early in the morning

113

or late at night – other walkers on the street
   seem figures of no reality, traffic
   is almost nonexistent – an empty

bus, a taxi with its off duty sign
   half lit so it says "off" in front and "duty"
   behind. i pass a locked church and a tavern

dark, and too forbiddingly peopled
   for limited courage to investigate.
   warily moving along, i pass an old

woman in rags dragging tattered shopping bags
   shouting obscenities to the vacant night
   behind me. i grow angry on her behalf

and think to be her champion, but there are
   not even phantoms to do battle with, not
   a windmill to tilt at! hell isn't other

people, but distances separating
   them even as they touch. hell begins at our
   umbilical cords and keeps growing.

suddenly, from a doorway, a shadow springs.
a cat shrieks. a chord from a zither rings.

Canto V

resembling my half-brother richard, but
   almost certainly the ghost of orson welles,
   his huge hand grips my shoulder as his words cut

into my brain... *son, i will show you all*
   of hell necessary for your improvement
   eternal... his voice floats as thru a hall.

i am hardly overjoyed at this meeting.
   "improve?" i ask. "on perfection?" he rattles
   his chains and cries out my name with such keening

114

as my mother used to in the darkest day
  of her self-disgust at bringing forth an
  adolescent monster. so i say, "ok,

direct me. but let's make it quick. the elrose
  superette closes in twenty minutes.
  eli'll think i'm stealing his change, and rose

will have that wounded look when i get back there
  that says how could you be so dastardly as
  to make a pregnant woman suffer one more

minute than she has to in this icy store?
  bristling, orson turns away toward the eifel
  tower, pulling back a cloth from the core

of his black coat, he wipes his grisly brow.
  he seems to count to ten and then says, *come on.*
  we've got to get this finished before cock crow.

"Cock crow? you mean sunrise? hey wait a minute.
  it can't be more than four or five in the
  afternoon." *there is no afternoon here, dimwit!*

only cock crow. i don't know why, but i
  suddenly feel sick. i begin puking flames.
  now i really worry. orson pinches my

arm, his claws digging into the flesh. *let's go.*
  stay in the center of the sidewalk. do not
  step on the cracks. touch no buildings or trees. no

stepping off curbs till the sign tells you to walk.
  "so what if i step on a crack or something?"
  a look of such agony! such a schreck!

"ok, ok. forget it. calm down.
so i'll stay off the cracks. Let's get it done!"

115

Canto VI

following closely behind my guide
   i behold great potholes in the streets
   and in each pothole a politician's head.

the head of edward koch, expatiating
   wildly with tongue nose and eyes, "how'm i doing?"
   he cries. i feel the poem degenerating.

through brooklyn's circles we spiral downward
   past gatherings of those who did violence
   to god and to man; and then of those who did

violence to no one. i think i see one
   such i knew sweeping out a store vestibule.
   it is lonesome john the freelance odd jobs man.

i say, "john, how came you here?" he says, *well,
   many were here who aren't now. they bought
   their way out.* "bought their way out of hell?"

"as above, so below" ... couldn't you have guessed, man?
   "i sure should've, john." then another poor soul
   tugs at my sleeve. it is a poet i'd known

on Gansevoort pier, salad days of '68.
   he blithely recites his master poem on
   being reborn into a jazz note.

i could stay listening to him for hours,
   but my guide cruelly moves me along. *this
   is the circle of the underachievers,*

he warns. *heed not their enticing tricks
   or be forever lost to the real world of
   progress and sophisticated robotics.*

then suddenly with a great orange glow
   the world begins burgeoning. it is sunrise
   in hades and i know it is time to go.

116

i find my truck bike where i'd chained it
  around a telephone pole, and ride it back
  to the elrose where eli and rose wait

to welcome me home from my arduous journey.
"What took you so long, fella? where's our money?"

EDEN

6 days marching brought me to this miserable ruin in this dark disgusting
wood to be watched like a laborator-
y animal the scrutiny's inter-
minable i howl over my own
cells' complexities my heart wishes
to escape to the other side of
my body there to beat against the
tide a drum of war against the inside under a tent of a willow
tree i sit and dig messages into the earth i don't care who reads them
or why i just leave them to leave them

WATERS: THREE POEMS FOR MY MOTHER
(October 31, 1986)

First Poem

My mother is dead. I am almost
certainly alive. The world is arranged
differently this evening than it was
the same time yesterday when my mother
was alive. I know Reagan and Gorbachev
are still alive and unable to do
that much about rearranging the world
for all their power. But my mother
has always rearranged the world with her
comparatively minor comings and
goings. Now she is gone. And presumably
will not return. Yet she has introduced
into my world permanent rearrangement.

Second Poem

Queen of your shut blue eyes in the bleak country
of solitude, I have seen the sorts of things
you wished me to look at, and have seen through
the mock opaqueness of it all. Usually
this would be enough to say. I could say it
and leave. People would want to wave to me
out their windows if only it didn't look so
lower class. I remember the time an
entire nation of immigrants turned out to
watch me dance. I danced a kazatska. Then
I dos-e-doed with a hippopotamus.
All the neighbors clapped their hands and stamped their feet
like there was nothing to be ashamed of.

Third Poem

Tonight, brown stars glare down dark stairwells, sink
into purple waters... going, going, gone.
The crowded shore is less crowded now by one.

SECRETS

when the joke springs up out of
the joker, a box
is empty, and waiting occupancy
waiting for the hermit jokester
this is the secret to davy jones' locker
to pandora's box
to the ark of the covenant
to the white house basement
to the sudden appearance of gopher tracks
on a tranquil lawn

on a tranquil morning, sitting under
a pear tree waiting for pears to
appear, i thought these thoughts
dimly conscious of a whirr in the air
i shivered slightly   you put a
shawl around my shoulders and gave me
a cup of hot chocolate
the whirr became louder and a
bright ball of fire appeared in the sky
when there should have been pears

you must hear the rest of my
revelations   i won't let you go
without sharing with you my
numbness, my perplexity, my
earnest desire for prosperity
at nobody's expense

YAK   ...FROM A BESTIARY
(for George Montgomery)

I once knew a yak whose heart stopped beating all at once.
We were on a camping trip up in the mountains
and I guess we climbed higher than we should have.
He was a big sweet old fellow with soft long hair that looked
golden in the sun and horns that he was so proud of, so proud
of...

THE COURIER

i ran all the way i almost
slipped on the gravel path i wanted to be the first with the news i
had learned before anyone what
it was everyone wanted to
know i knew i wanted to tell
i wanted to watch everyone's
eyes light with wonder and satisfaction or shut tight with fear and
melancholy i wanted to
see their jaws drop and their feet stamp
when i told them what they must hear
i wanted to feel their joy and
their wrath their misgivings and mis-
understandings when i addressed
each in his own tongue i couldn't wait
so i ran all the way the horizon kept receding but my
message and my knowledge urged me
on the skies were darkening street
lamps were beginning to come on
lights were being lit in the cot-
tages on the hills the villa-
ges i was racing to reach before it was too late to be the
first with the news but the hills kept
receding and i kept running
and kept running and keep running

ENEMIES

OF

TIME

DONALD LEV

Part Nine

Enemies of Time

FOG
for Enid

there was the fog of course
that altered our plans
the extra concern the peering through cotton smoke
exhausted me by the time we got to hurley
so we decided to get off the road at kingston, rest
awhile, and found this
french bistro
there in uptown kingston
you were beautiful, talked of
the brontës– maybe thinking of
fog on the moors –
how branwell actually published some poetry,
and charlotte fell in love with her belgian teacher –
over paté soup red wine
and this terrific chocolate concoction with
"angel hair" spider webs of sugar

and the owner gave us champagne on the house
because of our pleasure?
and we went out and the fog hadn't lifted

but it had.

WAITING ...

for what?
for the other shoe to drop?
for the tide to rise or fall?
for the image of the Void
to reproduce itself beneath my breast bone?

i have waited for happiness,
for surfeit of pleasure,
for surcease of sorrow.
i have waited for robins. i have waited for snow.

i wait for you now
so i won't have to wait alone.

THE ALTERNATIVE

I offered her a distinct
alternative. i said
"i am green, while other men
are pretty much clay colored.
i have four brains in constant
disharmony. i have feet
that are arguments, eyes
that are snow. i watch where
i go with pure malice,
but an ear for dialogue."

she said, "tell me, do you
come here often to this
restaurant where there are
no tables or chairs, nothing
but infinite flights of stairs?
and shouldn't we order wine?"

"of course!" i chimed, but under
my breath crustaceans crawled
wounded away to sea.

Hey, Man, is that the full moon up there?
I don't know, Man – I don't live in the neighborhood.

NOSTALGIA POEM: GREENWICH VILLAGE

I don't know what moon it was
I only know it's always the one and only moon but
what unique moon was it
alongside the tower, the cocked tower of
jefferson market library
the night in question
the night in question?
yes. the night in question
under its own unique moon.
unique to whom? a soul?
no matter. there was a sparkle
that still sparkles after all these years.
in yesteryear
it sparkled from under the el
but that was yesteryear
and the el and its beloved picturers are gone
but no more gone than
I or you or other heirs of Maurice,
the prodigious progeny of Bodenheim

who pass, casting reflected light
along eighth street or fourth street or bleecker street,
bathing one another, and all who walk
and walked and still their ghosts walk...

in that light i might see goldfinger, might see steve
tropp, george montgomery, bob white jr., barbara
holland, emilie glen, poor richard davidson; eunice
margot, julianne, rissa, ree, john payne, janet and
cicero; another might see kerouac, o'hara,
oppenheimer, blackburn, berrigan, bob vaughan;
another, ed blair, still another the great ginsberg,
or jack micheline, or armand schwerner whistling
on a ghostly reed.

but hey, the sky is lighting up

128

REUBEN
(A midrash for Enid)

I was an only child so briefly.
Then one by one those brothers came.
Squalling. Yelling. Demanding. Displacing.
More and more I withdrew.
I sought lands far away from these madmen.

But that weird little half-brother, I sort of liked.
Maybe because he had that other mother.
He was crazy, lived in his own world.
But why would anyone hate him?

I'm not the swiftest thinker.
But I'm glad I came up with that pit idea,
Which did save him.

And then he saved us!
Wow!

I'VE BEEN SIXTY

I've been sixty years old
A few days now
Though Enid and I are still celebrating.
Just ate a nice
three course dinner
At Joshua's with a bottle
Of California Chardonnay
That had a little kick to it
And I'm accompanying these perambulations
With some of my birthday sherry.

But I'm waiting for a warm woolen
Mantle of maturity to fall
Over my shoulders. I'm looking
for small young eyes
To upturn wide with respect
I want to walk my narrow,
Slightly rolling pathway
Down to the sea of death

With some dignity
But those dark clouds
Blowing past the sun
Say differently

(I might as well take
Up jogging, enter
The Boston Marathon)

I'm going up to bed now.
Tomorrow I will no longer
Be celebrating my 60th birthday.
Enough is enough!
Have I any last thoughts,
Observations?

DEVOLUTION

i am a frog sitting on a rock by the river euphrates.
(you have to start somewhere)

the earth is so fragrant and the river so full of life!

i am almost ready to march
as soon as i
can alter persona
not an easy thing to do
even in a poem there is much
twisting anguish

but i am a man now
in combat boots
ready to defend
my earth, my river

from whom? the insect, of course,
who invades every
peaceful stream with his
noisomeness

we have just fired off our cannon
there is a fragrance in the air of gunpowder
we have been misled we know
but we must follow step with step

to alter again is perhaps to find greater regret.

THE ROSENBERGS: SING SING PRISON,
JUNE 19, 1953, EVENING

he in his cage, just
outside her cage
their last scheduled three hours of life
swiped from them by
the religiously sensitive attorney-general
two birds, mated for life

he the stronger, really –
having sized things up historically;
knowing the only path he
has to take, he walks it.
she, too passionate to die...

For that reason, doesn't...

OVER BRIGHTON

they're repairing the ancient boardwalk
they have a portion of it blocked off
and carpenters are quite busy.
the rest of it is tramped by the many
varieties of humanity.
some skating or cycling, some jogging, most
gossiping, all enjoying God's vast blue skies.
i sit facing the sand facing the sea
in no better repair, certainly
and host to less variety
oh! And then there was the moon.
let's not forget the moon
that had begun rising like some sad and beautiful
warning out of Egypt.

THE DAY THE WORLD BEGAN
Rosh Hashana 5755, Near Woodstock, N.Y.

the earth, clay, alive with worms and stones
above are the stars, the moon
mostly hidden
it is the new moon nearest autumn
via the ancient lunar calendar
it marks the day the world began
a deer waited on the road, and as we approached
slowly, ran into the brush of apple trees in twilight
and the voice of god, muffled, began
whispering in the sweet cool air

there were boots caked with mud,
climbing an elegant stair
dove wings flapping just within range of hearing

there are important things
that must be done
deadlines to be met.

ON THE DAY OF ATONEMENT

Get ready. Your way. Nothing
in the room. The furniture
removed. Only the freshest
spider webs remain to
challenge the judgement upon
emptiness

Sad lives might
have poured out of you as from
a shoe box of unsorted
family photographs, were it
not for the emptiness

Oh, but surely something's
left inside! Even one
single scrap of passion
could provide your spiders
evidence in your defense.

Forgetfulness is your
defense against everything
but your apprehensions

which do not trouble you now,
but join this meditation.

TANTALUS AT THE SEDER

glatt kosher!
the newest restaurant in boro park
with seating for four hundred and an all new
revue from israel
complete with belly dancers and wisecrackers
on this ground
i walked
till i stumbled
looking for pockets
to escape in
what do i hate most about myself? my ignorance?
my bad faith? but the
evil son asks
what are you doing this for?

for myself, i answer. for my bad faith and my
ignorance.

fork in hand flowers in his eyes lordly mannered
tantalus stabs at a piece of gefilte fish &
bitter herb (he has resolved to be on good
behavior at this, his first family seder in many
centuries.)
of course the fish ball swims away and the
bitter herb sets off in a gallop after the spilt
milk of time and tantalus asks again as of old
what are you doing this for?
and we answer in total unison
for ourselves!
that god our father forbear eating us another year.

kings have a way with words that commoners are denied.
tantalus seems to whisper from somewhere deep
in the roots of his gonads
an elemental comment.
"all creation is feast for all creation save
one immortal
unconquerable idea:

the idea of Tantalus, the solitary inedible
element of the universe!"
and he stabbed again at a piece of lettuce,
watching it flit away with a
profound twinkle in his desperate, not
despairing eyes.
and pours the emptiness of a wine cup out in a
libation of contempt.

ON THE GENUINE

I want to write
Something genuine
As a sack of
Kosher chicken hearts
On sale at Nadler's

Not a poem at all
But an essay
On the competition between Nadler's and Feldman's
For the Empire of Brighton Beach
A town no longer big enough for two kosher butchers.

Feldman's with its counter backed by
Ruddy butchers in straw hats and
Traditional bloody white smocks
Chopping off your chosen chops
Before your eyes

Against Nadler's, whose butchers chopped
Behind walls
And bound their bright chops in demure plastic
To lay in well lit cases –
The clear winner

Putting Feldman's out of business
Putting genuine chicken hearts in
Clear plastic sacks.

FLUSHING MEADOWS

isn't this moment enough?
oh a waterway opens underneath a wooden bridge
and in emulation of others you bait hooks with dough
and try to fish
in one of two lakes or the little channel between them
that were created from the ancient flushing river
around 1939
i see a bucket and imagine it's being lowered
this is probably imaginary
there is this rambling wooden house, though
standing long vacant
supposedly belonging to Mayor LaGuardia, and thus
referred to as "the mayor's mansion" in which
generations of children played, and one probably
burned it to the ground
there is one dick downey
who doesn't remember as i do
his sitting in our vacant lot on Austin Street, with
his little pail and shovel, chanting, "I am digging my own
gra-a-ve"
who would know about this
i re-met him in Delaware County on the dark side of
the Catskills, he writes fiction
the moment, though, come back to the moment,
i am thinking of Mary Gordon's mother who had lived
in a nursing home and had no memory, which upset
Mary (in her book about her father) but didn't me...
what, i thought, is the use of having a memory
after all?
doesn't lack of memory make it easier to achieve
beat/buddhist ideal,
to live in the moment? and isn't this sufficient?
and if not, why not?
i mean, where does your memory get you
after you're dead?
maybe a head start on the next life according to
Mr. Rudolph Steiner, but now I'm just
running at the mouth
though i do ask myself
whether the fact that many poets in the past have also
known poverty
is any help in my case

"FOURTH AVENUE TYPEWRITERS"

is it the end of my
self

i see on a key
dangling

from the handle of
a metal-cased
portable typewriter-

manual
in an age
of speed
intelligence
and barely touching?

was it really left
in this ancient store
for repair?

ECCE HOMO

"Why are you doing this to me?"
The slight person in a pitch of anguish
addresses four large policemen
in the men's room
of Penn Station
They order him
to pull his pants up,
handcuff him,
and march him away.

COMMUNICATION

all i can hold in my two weak arms,
i toss across the abyss
to the side where
you stand alone under your ripped net

it is only a poem i send you
and i haven't worked on it very long

MORE DELI THAN DADA
in homage to Carl Solomon and Wallace Markfield

We, we sing.
We don't examine.

In another incarnation
Franz Kafka
lives on the internet
or, rather, finds himself
caught like an insect –
a prisoner of the internet

Poem:
I'll do anything
it takes to get into the
Norton Anthology!

Caught in a piece of time
a fossil in amber
a good luck charm dangling at the throat
of a terrible Goddess

Would it be a strain
to devote one line
to the sudden demise
of Princess Di?

What a shame!

There is no past.
There is nothing to disbelieve in.
All one needs is a justifying theme

HERE I AM

a dog
and a computer
associating with me
on terms i can only
pretend to fathom.
the computer was donated by people who pitied us.
it sits before us like a great stone god. It is silent
we do not dare approach it.

the dog is left in our care by a neighbor.
he has a Petey-like patch above his eye
and is therefore called Petey. he is
malamute, therefore part wolf. he likes us, we hope.

but i was thinking of a blues earlier... i forget now
which one, but it was one my friend Ian used to play.
and i pictured Ian young, bent gracefully
over his instrument. not yet splattered on a sidewalk
in forest hills queens after his second
leap from his sixth story apartment window.

then i seem to retaste wine i had drunk
not an hour ago in the warm restaurant
we had entered during a rainstorm

and I'm grateful.

YOU SLANT THE GLASS

You slant the glass to control the head –
My father taught me that.
I never learned the Morse Code
or to wiggle my ears –
But I do know how to pour a glass of beer.

OUR SABBATH

God & Mrs. God
(two blue candles in crimson holders),
the cosmos – a
flowered vase full of them –
and a bottle of
Spanish wine:
we meditate on multicultural pilpuls

ENEMIES OF TIME

"Personally, I
Loved Joe Stalin,"
She murmured into her third martini.

"Love *is* pain".

"Another thirty, forty years... it'll be all over."
Said by a bartender in Sunnyside Queens,
Circa 1954.

Me, I love to kill time.
God is going to hate me.

You are the enemy of time,
He'll say.
What can I say?

It's time, old man
    It's time
Your belly hairs
    Are turning white
It's time, old man
    It's time.

As time fades away
The young man hangs around Sheepshead Bay
Making his mother miserable
With his dyed hair
His attitude
His drag.
In a more merciful time
He would have been able to afford his own pad.
In a less merciful time he'd have had to.

WITHOUT ART LIFE IS NOTHING

There are corners of the universe
where the universe's people
conceal themselves
while all around them
monsters mate
and talk real estate

Just light and they're there
making you pay
for your moment

It's lucky I was born Jewish
it keeps a control over my
populistic instincts

I am an incarnation of Franz Kafka
domesticated
I've lost much of my fastidiousness,
wouldn't you say?

I'm hunting something

Poor me!
I'm one of the millions
of unrequited poets

I have no shared memories!

Above my chamber door
a bust of Bill Packard
nothing more

A poem is what
they don't tell you
on the evening news.

A LETTER FROM MY COUSIN'S DAUGHTER
for Valerie

My ancient aunt died.
She had in her possession
My few begrudging letters.
Seems she hadn't had much
Correspondence with anyone.
So I weep for her and her sad
Sisters and brothers, now
Probably all gone –
My own mother among them –
Children of sad practitioners
Of ephemera
Cast upon these shores
Some hundred years ago –
Each unhappy child
Learning lessons of poverty
Deeply unique to herself,
Each responding with protest
Likewise deeply unique.

They lived long these siblings,
Except for the one murdered
By her husband... But their children
Tend to die young.

Their grandchildren are not numerous.
I am grateful to have heard from one.

THOUGHTS ON ALLEN GINSBERG

the uncle sam hat
above the face
that bore his name
like a national banner:
was his language the same as longfellow's?
shakespeare's? robert e lee's?
ezra pound's?
i've been writing poems since 1958
not much like his my lines few,
jagged, scattershot with rhymes and assonances
but he for me somehow was always
a permitting presence.
i'd scan the universe for hints on how
a jewish dropout in america, reluctant to leave queens,
makes poems:
the way ads read, ferlinghetti's lines, dylan
thomas's resonant consonants, the way things
looked stoned.
and his occasional pronouncements: e.g.,
on the size of one's notebook.
he was candor incarnate.
i am oblique, subterranean, but i hope still truthful.
his *kaddish*, to me, is the greatest american poem,
pure candor
a type of work i couldn't begin.
but today we – all – like and unlike – write
in the light of him.

JEWISH NEW YEAR

no one has been counting.
we have been lost in swirling seas of grasses
for some time now –
during an eternity of twilight.
we have just been asked to rise by a small man
in a white skullcap.
we do, but lose sight of him
behind rows of risen tall people.
we think he has something to say, but
cannot hear his voice over a racket of police car sirens
emanating from the roadside.
the year advanced towards equinox –
a not altogether inauspicious beginning.

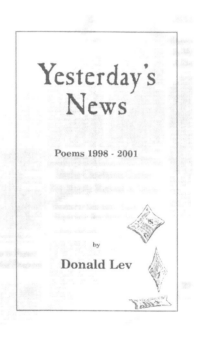

Yesterday's News

Poems 1998 - 2001

by

Donald Lev

Part Ten

Yesterday's News

THE THIRD ADAM

Catapulted into twilight – a blessing impossible to welcome,
Under darkening skies that suggest nothing;
Under beginning starlight that promises no destiny;
Under umbrella trees that neglect to shelter
Small, undefined, yet

Unperplexed, he
Scurries about the wide, overgrown, pathless world,
Now mostly of his creating. His little hand
With its still opposable thumb grips the mouse
as he searches for one more redemption somewhere
   in the virtual
infinite web.

NIGHTMARE

A fitfully sleeping world turns and tosses in nightmare.
Befanged amphibians are part of it. Deranged humanity as well.
Intimations of cosmologists combine with ambitions
    of nihilists.
A suicide sits in a waiting room.

A suicide sits in the waiting room of Grand Central Station.
He has a rather large piece of luggage between his legs. He
    begins to nod.
Scenes from a dismal, displaced childhood dovetail within
    his consciousness
Like a pack of dirty playing cards.

Like a pack of dirty playing cards his life unfolds, melds.
All of the blows, the harangues, the rapes, the accusations,
    the dizzying strains of lives
Bled into the dust of a barbed courtyard fan out before him.
The clock of his revenge ticks off the seconds.

The clock of his revenge ticks off seconds of the old
    century as we
Count up bottles of Champagne purchased in advance
    of demand
To be certain of supply for our millennial celebrations.
It is not we who turn and toss in nightmare.

WHAT WAS IT?

What was it? A rose? A little fluffy white cat reflected in
    a pane of glass?
Where do storms begin? Show me some patch of ocean to
sink
    my prayers in.
Reveal to me the graffiti scribbled on the void
The smudge of sunlight I am to understand.

I am to understand, am I? Every bulge and bend in the
universe, each
Catastrophic event in the bleak and starry seas
Surrounding my pitiable privacy must become known to
me
While my heart's whole and my walnut brain's uneaten,

And my dust's yet undistributed over the dance floor of
    the crowded discotheque of Time?
Here, Kitty, the sea's still calm. Ah, the fragrance
Of this cut rose with an aspirin to sustain it, and a
Very wee fragment of the once huge brain of Einstein!

PARABLE

The scent of snuffed candle follows me
Through the needle's eye of poetry.

LITERATUS

There was a trained intelligence!
Words flew out of his bright blue eyes.
Sentences raged like static electricity from his wild hair.
Paragraphs rolled over his ample belly
Like a long wide flowery necktie.

How he made the rest of us sweat!
Even the gamblers in the next room
Cashed in their chips and began to take notes.

Even my mother's parakeet chattered his praises
And refused to have its cage covered
Till the master had bidden all goodnight.

I found myself breaking out in a cold sweat
And racing into the chilly street.

What I didn't expect was to hear his footsteps behind me,
And his voice, crisp as a silver dollar moon beam,
Warning me.

A SNAKE
for Enid Dame

A snake grew out of the wild grasses by the side of the
Street I was walking and slithered across my path
Comfortably curling itself upon the sidewalk's warm
    flagstone.

What's the rush? it seemed to say – of course it did not
    speak, but
Eyed me eloquently as only a reptile can.

My horse bridled, though I sat no horse, and I
Reined mightily to control him.
I felt a cry from deep within his animal fear;
I cleared my throat to stifle it.

The snake was multihued, from a silvery underbelly to the
Green black orange and red upper scaling – I know
    my nomenclature's
Imprecise – I'm not in the habit of observing serpents –
    though perhaps
I should be.

Could it have observed my sudden embarrassment,
    my guilt –
        which perhaps
Transformed my terror into something else?

It fixed me in its beady gaze like a drunk about to make a
Drunkenly dignified pronouncement on life morality
    and friendship.
I stiffened
Waited for the attack.
The stab of primordial wisdom, the blinding light from
under eons of
Igneous rock.

My life paraded before me in its underwear.
It needed a haircut and a beardtrim.

160

It kept consulting its wristwatch
And searching frantically for a way out.

I was not bitten that day or ever, to date.
The next day brought its solaces
And the day after that brought its
And so on and so forth...
To date.

That there is a message I must hear,
I fear.

ON THE RONDOUT
Kingston, NY

We walked along a kind of raft way
Running several feet between the marina and the shore.
On one side were handsome motor boats, on the other
Floating dead fish.

Then we went back up the hill for a beer.

We returned to the shore in time to hear
The girl singer with a small jazz combo ask for requests.
She said "we'll try our best but the band only knows
    four tunes"
There were too few people gathered to show any
    great appreciation
For the joke, so they started to play.

They weren't bad.

This was the Fourth of July.

Some old WWII vets had been on the radio
Kvetching about not getting their medals.

What a terrible way to report the above!
This was truly a horror. These guys were in the
Heart of the fighting on the island of Saipan.
They'd all been wounded and their outfit was decimated
And they were recalling tremendous feats of heroism
On the part of many who never returned
But this general, to cover up his own mistakes,
Branded these men cowards!

They were holding a reunion in Troy.

We saw no fireworks, heard no firecrackers.

OK

Workday tomorrow

End of report.

I forgot about the Chinese meal we had uptown. It was good.

FRAGMENT ON WATER

Does water fit the argument?
I see it in my palms
I feel it pouring down the back of my neck
I drink it
I bathe in it
My soul is cleansed by it
A leak some places can result in a big water bill
I stepped into a ditch filled with it, not good
Aren't we humans mostly water and a little ash?
Did I get that right?
The earth is mostly water and a little dirt
Right?
They think maybe they found some on Mars?
Like water's a big subject
Maybe too big for me to tackle
Like life, which I tackle often anyway, or
Death, about which I'm a minor expert
But this is water
This is "blood, sweat, and tears"
This is Jesus in Gethsemane sweating blood
This is the iceberg that did in the Titanic
This is the ocean out of which someone wants to
Bring up the Titanic
Whose morals are being questioned
Water and morality
Water in the mideast a big subject
I'm not equipped to discuss
I should have majored in geology in college, maybe
Gotten into hydrology
All you needed to do was memorize a bunch of rocks
I counseled my friend Rudy to do it, and he did
He's a practicing geologist today, whatever that is
I don't know whether he's a hydrologist, though
We *are* discussing water
Does that bring us to discuss skies and clouds and
Rain and snow and bridges over rivers and
All the ships at sea
And urine
And pus

164

But now I've gone too far
A nice little running brook
To delight our mind
With guys in high boots flycasting for trout
Lets have a fish dinner;
Gefilte fish maybe, or lobster
Clam chowder, tasting of oceans
Brighton Beach, Coney Island
Rockaway
The Sound
The river Rhine
The Rhine maidens, the Sirens
The cute mermaids
Surf Avenue, Nathan's
The Aquarium
Is it better to take a bath or a shower?
Whew this is becoming a very long poem
But water is a deep, deep subject
Maybe it would have been better to
Leave it alone.

DECADENCE

This is about decadence:
The twentyfirst century when everything runs down.
Where are the princely beings
That met at Yalta, that founded NATO,
That buried the Axis finally and fully?
One Empire rules,
Its legions police the world
While little or nothing is produced within its borders.
The Modernists are gone, the Beats are almost gone
The schools of poetry left are the MFA's – the necktied
MFA's and
The unnecktied MFA's; and the school of poets who
harangue each other
From keystones of great bridges.
The age of the clone is here
And distance learning
And CVS
And steroids on Olympus
And chips.

A MEDITATION

Listening for anything
One bird might say to another
A couple of sparrows or wrens
Hopping about a bush,
A pair of jays or pigeons
A gull a tern
Canaries in a petshop
What have they got to say?
I'd like to gain the confidence of
Rocks, trees, butterflies, worms
Remember Bob & Ray's "horrible record"
"The Sound of Worms"?
I do, and I wish I didn't.
What is anybody on earth thinking?
What am I thinking, and why?
A child and his father were caught
In a crossfire of angry residents and soldiers in Gaza.
The child died.
A cameraman caught it all for French TV
What was anyone truly thinking?

I am listening for anything
One politician might say to another.

ARRANGEMENT

There's no hurry.
Something will take possession.
Already someone is aiming a tool
At the workings of materials
As yet unconceived.
But there is no hurry.
The night hasn't far to go
But the dawn rises slow.
No hurry. No hurry.
The cortege will wait
Till everyone's ready.

PICTURE

Picture upon this wooden stage
As wide as an owl's peripheral vision,
As deep as a cat
Perceives:
Cowboys, Indians, and knights in armor
Mounted on stallions as beautiful as mountains.
They are roping they are singing they are pitching
Javelins into the skies.
You and I, we
Climb up with them
And begin to tapdance.
Don't worry, I'll teach you how, I say.
You say, don't worry just watch what I do
You follow me
Then I follow you
Till the orchestra's last notes die out.

STORM

Help! The sky is filled with falling books!
The sun is hidden by them.
They are crashing wildly all over the prairie destroying
    farmhouses,
Barns, stables and radio stations.
They are flattening new crops, destroying whole
    agra businesses.
Chickencoops are crushed. Feathers fly among the pages.
When and where will it end? What will it mean
When all the land lies quiet under blankets of
    unread books?

THE MAGIC OF COMMERCIAL PHOTOGRAPHY

The garbage can inverted upon which the model sits
   crosslegged and beautiful
Is also beautiful.
Steely gray light plays behind the scene as I begin
   turning the page.

SHORE

There is no place to rest.
There is a hope, placed well inside the chest
And not brought out every day, not even every
   Sabbath day.
Stones cold and sharp suggest new creations, possibilities.
Lapping waters, what do they suggest?
The salt in the air, the cries of sea birds.
Here is where I've built my nest.
Here is where I wait helplessly!

WHAT DO YOU FIX HERE?

What do you fix here?
Everything.
I have a broken rib.
That too.
I have taken a handful of rocks with me to this interview.
I think I want to toss them at a target.
Or drop them on
A nice shiny table.
Outside the Bowery Repair Mission
Men are gathering.
One of them sits on the sidewalk, his back
Against the wall of the mission.
He has just had his crutch stolen.
He wonders whether to be angry.

INDEPENDENCE DAY

The banks are closed today.
It is a holiday.
We should take a basket of ice out
To the tennis courts where
Some strangers are being executed.
We shall celebrate
Some anniversary or other.
This is the weather for it!

This is the weather for anything.
My necktie just caught in the wind
And spun me like a top for almost twenty seconds
While I watched a treeful of sparrows watch me.

Yet I am free!
Don't let my chains or my hangdog expression
Fool you
I did not need to be here.
I forced myself.

LOOK UNDER ANY SHOE

Maybe it's pinned under something.
The wheels of the car, maybe.
Or that rock that seems to be in the way of everything but
Nobody ever has the time to remove it.
Maybe it's under the foundation of the house like a
    skull under a segment of the
Great Wall of China.
Maybe it's in China.
Maybe it's been swallowed by somebody accused of spying.
Maybe it's stuck to the bottom of the pole of a
    beach umbrella.
We'll have to wait till evening to have a look.
Maybe it's on the bottom of one of my shoes.
No. It isn't.
Well, that is one clue.

A QUICK TRIP

A quick trip up a tree to see what gods still live there
Then down again in time for high tea
With herrings sherry those unusual little biscuits, and
Lots of whiskey.
We have had a profoundly good time here in the
   oldest country.
We are feeling quite refreshed, and not as nearly
   depressed as
We would ordinarily wish to be.
We'll scribble it all down,
Then see what there was to see.

SCENE FROM A MARRIAGE

So precarious!
Two tipsy piles of books
At the edge of the dresser,
Her reading glasses tucked
In between them.

On my side,
An even tipsier pile
Threatens from the night table.

MEMOIR

The little girl sits small on the big chair with all the doilies.
The grandfather clock strikes one.
There are canaries in a cage that sing.
There is a clear sky outside clean windows.

Kate Smith is on the radio.
She is bantering with Ted Collins and selling something.
She will tell a story about a little dogwood tree,
Then sing God Bless America.

Irving Berlin is uncorking a bottle of champagne
In another corner of the big living room
The radio program has not yet been interrupted
By the death of President Roosevelt,

And our bombers still fly over the white cliffs of Dover,
Which is how it is and should always be.

ON THE DESTRUCTION OF THE WORLD TRADE CENTER
September 11th, 2001

All the papers have
Yesterday's news.

HARD

It was hard just going there.
Seeing those same people I saw
Hundreds of times before
When going there was no easier.
I'd have to keep my hat on, and my
Shirt buttoned to the top and my
Necktie tightly tied.
Always the same necktie full of stripes.
It was hard going there because my shoes
Which always had to be new and hurt
Had to be highly shined.
All this to ride a hot fumy bus
Three quarters of an hour
Just to be there.

Only to be there.

Only to be certain to be there.

9/23/01

I want to die in
    Union Square
And be immediately
    resurrected there
Among the candles,
The steel bands,
The chanting buddhists

The Americans!

WHEELS

Wheels churn helplessly in unforgiving mud.
It has been raining off and on for almost forty days
And I am soaked by rain tears and snot
Running from my nose and sweat welling up from my
rubber encased body as I struggle with all
I am given in life to struggle with.
There is a rainbow and a dove pictured on a
Postage stamp somewhere on my person perhaps
In my wallet, and now probably
Too drenched to use
On the letter I had tried to address to my
Better angels begging them to calm me down
Sufficiently to accept survival as my due
And grief as a conclusion I am still coming to.

Alphabetical Index of Poems

185

Bibliography

The poems in this volume have been reprinted from the following collections:

HYN and Other Poems, New York: privately printed, generosity of Ree Dragonette, 1968.

A STRING OF BEADS for Maxine, New York: Bowery View Press, 1971.

Peculiar Merriment, New York: Home Planet Publications, 1973.

Intercourse With the Dead, Brooklyn: Downtown Poets Co-op, 1980.

Footnotes, Merrick, NY: Cross Cultural Communications, 1982.

There is Still Time, Providence: The Poet's Press, 1986.

The Days of the Easter Bunny, Claryville, NY: CRS Outloudbooks, 1990.

Twentieth Century Limited, New Brunswick: Iniquity Press/Vendetta Books, 1992.

Twilight, CRS Outloudbooks, 1995.

There is Still Time (new expanded edition), Weehawken, NJ: The Poet's Press, 1998.

Enemies of Time, West Orange, NJ: Warthog Press, 2000.

Yesterday's News, CRS Outloudbooks, 2002.